The River's Journey

Kate McGough

Have you ever seen a river?
A river is a large stream
of flowing water. This river
is the Mississippi River.
It flows through the United States.

3

Look at this map of the United States. It shows where the Mississippi River begins and ends. Let's follow the Mississippi River on its long journey.

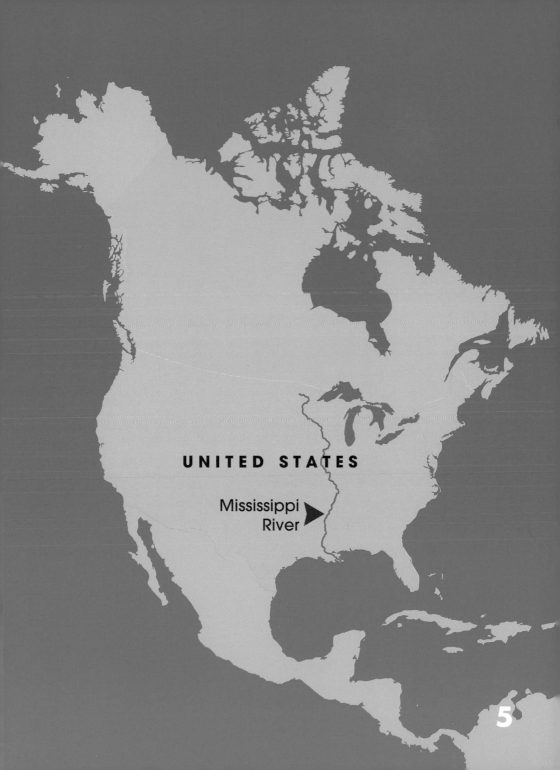

UNITED STATES

Mississippi ▶
River

Where a river begins is called its source. The Mississippi River begins in a lake in Minnesota. It starts out as a small, clear stream.

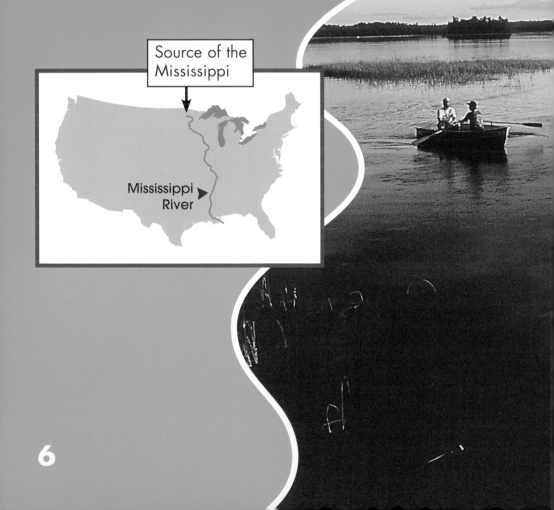

Source of the Mississippi

Mississippi River

Other small streams flow into the Mississippi River. The river gets bigger and faster. At the Falls of St. Anthony, the river flows through locks. Locks raise or lower the water, helping boats to travel on the river.

The Falls of St. Anthony

Mississippi River

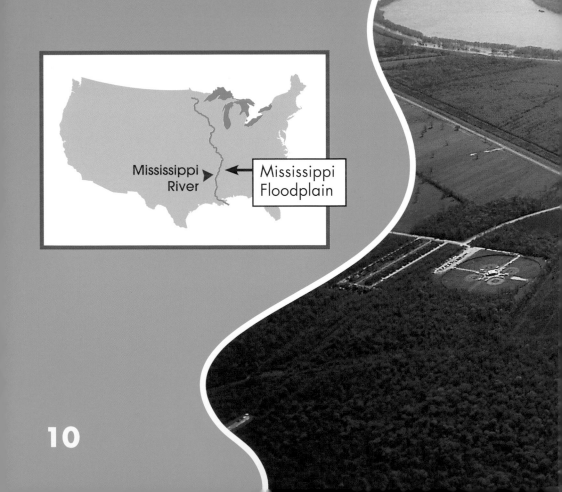

The Mississippi River flows down to lower land. It flows more slowly over the flat land. It begins to wind back and forth. The flat land around the river is called its floodplain.

Mississippi River

Mississippi Floodplain

The river slows near the end of its journey.
It drops the mud and soil that it collected
further upstream. The mud and soil
form new land called a delta.
The Mississippi Delta is very large.

The end of a river is called its mouth. A river's mouth empties into another body of water. The Mississippi River empties into the Gulf of Mexico. The river's long journey has ended.

Mississippi River

Gulf of Mexico

15

Glossary

delta   new land formed by the mud and soil dropped by a river

floodplain   the flat land around a river

lock   a series of gates used to raise or lower the water so that boats can travel along

mouth   the end of a river

river   a large stream of flowing water

source   the beginning of a river

stream   a small river